LIFE WITH
AUTISM

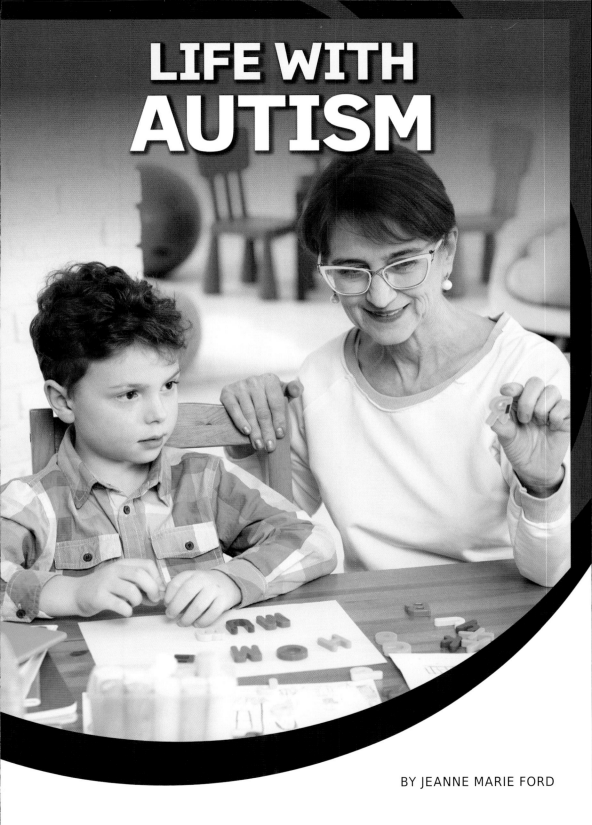

BY JEANNE MARIE FORD

Published by The Child's World®
1980 Lookout Drive • Mankato, MN 56003-1705
800-599-READ • www.childsworld.com

Content Consultant: Karen Pierce, Ph.D., Co-Director,
University of California San Diego Autism Center of Excellence

Photographs ©: Shutterstock Images, cover, 1, 5 (left), 5 (right); Kathy Hutchins/
Shutterstock Images, 6; William T. Wade Jr./Splash News/Newscom, 8; Wave
Break Media/Shutterstock Images, 10; iStockphoto, 12; Darrylee Cohen/AdMedia/
Newscom, 14; Phil McCarten/AP Images, 16; Eric Sucar/The Daily Messenger/AP
Images, 18; Apega/MCT/Newscom, 20

ISBN 9781503825062
LCCN 2017959682

Printed in the United States of America
PA02375

TABLE OF
CONTENTS

FAST FACTS

- Autism **spectrum** disorder (ASD) causes changes in the brain that affect behavior and communication. Some people with ASD have such mild symptoms that they are never **diagnosed**. Others never learn to speak. They may need help with the most basic daily tasks. They may have severe **learning disabilities**.

- People with ASD often have trouble with social skills. They tend to avoid eye contact. They might prefer to repeat certain movements and **routines**. Many people with ASD are also sensitive to sights, sounds, and smells.

- Doctors do not know exactly what causes ASD. There is probably more than one cause. In some people, **abnormalities** in specific **genes** have been found. ASD can run in families. Approximately one out of every 68 children in the United States today has ASD.

- There is no cure for ASD. But speech and behavioral therapy can improve how people with ASD communicate with others.

Boys are nearly five times more likely to be diagnosed with ASD than girls.

lorful.
more colorful.
mo
more
lorful.
colorful.
mor
more
lorful.
e colorful.

Chapter 1

TEMPLE GRANDIN

Three-year-old Temple Grandin did not speak. When she was unhappy, she screamed. When she was told to do something she didn't like, she threw a **tantrum**. She chewed puzzle pieces. She flung any object within her reach.

The world around Temple was too loud. Smells were too strong. Clothes were too scratchy. Temple would sit for hours and spin coins or sift sand through her fingers, studying each grain. She often seemed to be in her own world.

Temple grew up during the 1950s. At that time, doctors did not know much about autism. They did not know how intelligent people with autism could be.

◀ **Temple Grandin attended the Emmys in 2010 when a film based on her life was nominated for awards.**

▲ **Temple poses with her book, *The Autistic Brain*, during a book tour in 2013.**

Doctors gave Temple's parents little hope that she could lead a full life.

Temple's mother found a speech therapist. The therapist taught Temple how to talk. At the age of five, Temple started kindergarten at her local school.

Temple had trouble relating to other people. Her best friends were imaginary ones. Today, Temple believes that her autism helped her relate to animals. She enjoyed spending time with the animals on her grandparents' farm.

In high school, Temple decided science would be her life's focus. She went on to graduate from high school and college. She became a professor of animal science.

"If I could snap my fingers and be non-autistic, I would not," she said in a lecture in 1993. "Because then I wouldn't be me."

ON THE SPECTRUM

ASD affects people in different ways. Some people have mild or moderate ASD. Others have more severe ASD. People with mild ASD, such as Temple Grandin, are usually very intelligent but may be socially **awkward**. Scientists believe that many important figures in history, such as scientist Albert Einstein, may have had mild forms of ASD.

Chapter 2

AMIN

Ten-year-old Amin had severe autism. He moved slowly in the morning. His mom helped him wash his face, brush his teeth, and get dressed. He ate pancakes every day for breakfast because he liked his morning activities to be predictable.

Amin looked forward to the routines at school that helped him learn. Even though he didn't speak or read, he understood a lot. Therapists worked with Amin during the day. They helped him follow classroom rules and control his outbursts when he got frustrated.

Amin rode the bus home each day after school. His mom met him at the front door of their house. Sometimes he was happy and wanted to be tickled.

◀ **Kids with ASD often follow routines, such as eating the same food for breakfast each morning.**

On other days, he came home crying because he was tired, hungry, or sad. He searched immediately for a chain of metal beads. He twirled the chain between his fingers. This **stimming** behavior helped comfort and calm him.

After school, Amin spent two more hours working with therapists. Sometimes he practiced buttoning a shirt or putting his clothes in the laundry. But Amin's favorite activity was going to the store to practice buying a candy bar.

Later, Amin snuggled on the couch with his grandma. They watched TV shows together. Finally, it was time to rest after a long, full day.

◄ **Kids with ASD often need specialized therapists to help them build communication skills.**

Chapter 3

DEREK PARAVICINI

Three-year-old Derek Paravicini did not care about most toys. The only toy he wanted to play with was a small keyboard. Derek had severe autism. He was also blind. He had never seen anyone play a piano. He didn't know that pianists used their fingers to press the keys. Derek karate-chopped the keyboard with his whole hand. He used his elbows and his nose. Suddenly, his sister realized he was playing a song they had just heard in church.

Adam Ockelford, Derek's piano teacher, soon realized how musically talented Derek was. The first time Derek met Ockelford, Derek was eager to get to the piano.

◀ Derek Paravicini's musical talent has made him well-known around the world.

▲ **Derek has performed at many fundraisers and charity events.**

He shoved Ockelford off of the piano bench because he was so excited to play. Derek attacked the instrument with his arms and elbows.

Ockelford soon discovered that Derek could play any song he had ever heard. He could imitate any style of playing. Derek had a hard time communicating with words. But he learned that he could communicate through music.

Today, Derek has given hundreds of concerts. He has sold out auditoriums. He has raised millions of dollars for charities. Some of these fundraisers help other people with autism or blindness.

Derek does not know his right hand from his left. He is not sure how long he has been playing piano or how old he is. But he has touched many people's lives with his musical gift.

SAVANTS

Savant syndrome (sahv-AHNT SIN-drohm) is a condition in which a person with a mental disability has extraordinary skills in a particular area. Not all savants have ASD. But savant syndrome is more common among people with ASD than among the general population. Some savants, such as Derek, may be musicians or artists. Some may have amazing abilities to calculate numbers or dates. Scientists are trying to discover what changes in the brain cause people to become savants.

Chapter 4

JASON McELWAIN

Jason McElwain lived for basketball. When he did not make his high school's team, he became a student manager. He attended every game in a suit and tie. After every practice, he found a court and practiced dribbling and shooting baskets.

As a young child, Jason was diagnosed with severe autism. He didn't speak until he was five years old. He ate mainly canned spaghetti and baby food because he didn't know how to chew.

Sports helped Jason connect with his older brother, Josh. He grew more social and confident as he played.

The high school basketball coach let Jason suit up for the last game of the season. The team worked hard.

◄ Jason McElwain shoots for a basket during the last game of Greece Athena High School's season in 2006.

▲ **Jason (left) attended a fundraiser in 2008 with his mother, Debbie (right).**

The players wanted to get a huge point lead so the coach would put Jason in the game.

Jason's jersey hung on his skinny frame as he ran onto the court. A teammate tossed him the ball. He shot and missed. He shot again. But again, he missed. Then he made a basket, and another. The crowd went wild.

With only four minutes left to play, Jason racked up 20 points. It was the best day of his life.

There would be more good days. After he graduated, Jason continued to coach for his high school team. He became a competitive marathon runner. He cowrote a book about his experiences growing up with autism, and he made speeches around the country. Today, Jason continues to inspire young people to believe that they can make a difference if they follow their passions.

THINK ABOUT IT

- How might an autistic person experience the world differently from a non-autistic person?
- Think about your favorite game or sport. How could you adapt it for an autistic person?
- How could you be a better friend to someone you know who has autism?

GLOSSARY

abnormalities (ab-nor-MAL-i-teez): Abnormalities are characteristics that differ from what is expected. Gene abnormalities cause many diseases and disorders.

awkward (AWK-wurd): Someone who feels awkward is uncomfortable in certain situations. People with autism often feel awkward at parties or in large groups of people.

diagnosed (dye-uhg-NOHSD): A patient is diagnosed with an illness or a disorder when a doctor identifies the patient's symptoms. More boys than girls are diagnosed with autism.

genes (JEENZ): Genes are located within the body's cells, and they determine which traits are passed down to a child from parents. In some cases, a person's genes determine whether they have autism.

learning disabilities (LURN-ing diss-uh-BIL-uh-teez): Learning disabilities affect the way a person learns and can cause extra challenges in school. Some people with autism have severe learning disabilities.

routines (roo-TEENZ): Routines are patterns of behavior that are followed often. People with autism tend to thrive on routines.

spectrum (SPEK-truhm): A spectrum is a range over which something is measured. Autism spectrum disorder covers a range of autistic symptoms, from mild to severe.

stimming (STIM-ing): Stimming means making repeated movements or sounds. People with autism often find comfort from stimming.

tantrum (TAN-truhm): A tantrum is a dramatic expression of temper and frustration, especially in a young child. When she was young, Temple Grandin communicated that she did not want to do something by throwing a tantrum.

TO LEARN MORE

Books

Barghoorn, Linda. *Temple Grandin: Pioneer for Animal Rights and Autism Awareness*. New York, NY: Crabtree Publishing, 2017.

Frenz, Florida. *How to Be Human: Diary of an Autistic Girl*. Berkeley, CA: Creston Books, 2013.

Verdick, Elizabeth, and Elizabeth Reeve. *The Survival Guide for Kids with Autism Spectrum Disorders (and Their Parents)*. Minneapolis, MN: Free Spirit Publishing, 2012.

Web Sites

Visit our Web site for links about autism:

childsworld.com/links

Note to Parents, Teachers, and Librarians: We routinely verify our Web links to make sure they are safe and active sites. So encourage your readers to check them out!

SELECTED BIBLIOGRAPHY

"Autism Spectrum Disorder (ASD)." *Centers for Disease Control and Prevention*. US Department of Health and Human Services, n.d. Web. 21 Dec. 2017.

Diagnostic and Statistical Manual of Mental Disorders, Fifth Edition. Arlington, VA: American Psychiatric Association, 2013. Print.

Grandin, Temple, and Richard Panek. *The Autistic Brain: Thinking across the Spectrum*. Boston, MA: Houghton Mifflin, 2013. Print.

INDEX

ABOUT THE AUTHOR

Jeanne Marie Ford is an Emmy-winning TV scriptwriter who holds an MFA in Writing for Children from Vermont College. She has written numerous children's books and articles and also teaches college English. She lives in Maryland with her husband and two children.